Bangin' Shrimp Delights

A Cookbook for Irresistible Bang Bang Shrimp Creations

While every precaution has been taken in the preparation of this book, the publisher assumes no responsibility for errors or omissions, or for damages resulting from the use of the information contained herein.

BANGIN' SHRIMP DELIGHTS

First edition. March 7, 2024.

Copyright © 2024 Jose Maria.

ISBN: 979-8224627479

Written by Jose Maria.

Table of Contents

Jose Maria

❖ Introduction

A. What is Bang Bang Shrimp?

Bang Bang Shrimp is a delectable seafood dish renowned for its crispy texture and explosive flavors. The dish typically features shrimp coated in a creamy, spicy sauce, offering a tantalizing combination of sweetness and heat. The name "Bang Bang" originates from the explosive burst of flavors that dance on your palate with each bite.

B. Origin and History of Bang Bang Shrimp

The origins of Bang Bang Shrimp trace back to the culinary scene of the United States, particularly to the vibrant coastal city of Miami, Florida. While the exact inventor of this iconic dish remains a topic of debate, many attribute its creation to a seafood restaurant in the early 1990s. Over time, Bang Bang Shrimp garnered widespread popularity, becoming a staple in the menus of numerous seafood eateries across the country.

C. Why Bang Bang Shrimp is Popular

Bang Bang Shrimp has captured the hearts and taste buds of food enthusiasts worldwide for several reasons. Its irresistible combination of crispy shrimp and creamy, tangy sauce offers a delightful sensory experience. Additionally, the dish's versatility allows for endless variations, from tacos and salads to pizzas and sushi rolls, making it suitable for various culinary preferences and occasions. Furthermore, its easy preparation and bold flavors make it an ideal choice for both casual dining and special gatherings, further cementing its status as a beloved dish in the culinary landscape.

Chapter (1) Getting Started with Bang Bang Shrimp

A. Ingredients Overview

To embark on your Bang Bang Shrimp culinary journey, you'll need a handful of essential ingredients:

- Shrimp: Opt for fresh or frozen shrimp, preferably large in size, peeled, and deveined.
- Cornstarch: Used to coat the shrimp before frying, creating a crispy texture.
- Egg: Whisked with the cornstarch to help bind it to the shrimp.
- Oil: Suitable for frying the shrimp until golden and crispy.
- Bang Bang Sauce: A blend of mayonnaise, sweet chili sauce, and hot sauce, providing the signature creamy-spicy flavor.
- Optional Garnishes: Fresh cilantro, sliced green onions, sesame seeds, or lime wedges to enhance presentation and flavor.

B. Essential Cooking Equipment

To prepare Bang Bang Shrimp to perfection, ensure you have the following cooking equipment on hand:

- Deep Fryer or Skillet: To fry the shrimp until crispy and golden brown.
- Tongs: For safely flipping and removing the shrimp from the oil.
- Mixing Bowls: To coat the shrimp in cornstarch and egg mixture and to prepare the Bang Bang sauce.
- Whisk: For whisking together the ingredients of the Bang Bang sauce.
- Paper Towels: To drain excess oil from the fried shrimp.

C. Tips for Cooking Perfect Bang Bang Shrimp

Achieving restaurant-quality Bang Bang Shrimp at home is easier than you think with these helpful tips:

1. Prep Shrimp Properly: Ensure shrimp are thoroughly cleaned, peeled, and deveined before cooking to remove any grit or impurities.
2. Maintain Oil Temperature: Keep the oil temperature consistent around 350°F (175°C) to ensure crispy shrimp without becoming greasy.
3. Work in Batches: Fry shrimp in batches to prevent overcrowding the pan, which can result in uneven cooking and soggy shrimp.
4. Drain Excess Oil: After frying, transfer the shrimp to a paper towel-lined plate to drain excess oil, maintaining their crispy texture.
5. Coat Shrimp Evenly: Coat shrimp evenly in cornstarch and egg mixture before frying to ensure a uniform and crispy crust.
6. Serve Immediately: Enjoy Bang Bang Shrimp immediately after frying for the best texture and flavor experience.

Chapter (2) Classic Bang Bang Shrimp Recipes

A. Traditional Bang Bang Shrimp

Ingredients:

- 1 pound large shrimp, peeled and deveined
- 1/2 cup cornstarch
- 2 eggs, beaten
- Oil for frying
- 1/2 cup mayonnaise
- 1/4 cup sweet chili sauce
- 1 tablespoon hot sauce (adjust to taste)
- Optional garnishes: chopped green onions, sesame seeds, lime wedges

Instructions:

1. In a mixing bowl, combine mayonnaise, sweet chili sauce, and hot sauce. Stir well to combine, then set aside to use as dipping sauce.
2. Heat oil in a deep fryer or skillet to 350°F (175°C).
3. In a separate bowl, coat shrimp evenly with cornstarch, shaking off any excess.
4. Dip cornstarch-coated shrimp into beaten eggs, ensuring they are well coated.
5. Carefully place shrimp into the hot oil in batches, frying for 2-3 minutes or until golden brown and crispy.
6. Remove shrimp from oil using a slotted spoon and drain on a paper towel-lined plate.
7. Serve hot with the prepared Bang Bang sauce and optional garnishes. Enjoy immediately!

B. Bang Bang Shrimp Tacos
Ingredients:

- Cooked Bang Bang Shrimp (from the Traditional Bang Bang Shrimp recipe)
- 8 small flour or corn tortillas
- Shredded lettuce
- Diced tomatoes
- Sliced avocado
- Crumbled cotija or shredded cheddar cheese
- Lime wedges
- Chopped cilantro (optional)

Instructions:

1. Warm tortillas in a skillet or microwave until soft and pliable.
2. Fill each tortilla with shredded lettuce, diced tomatoes, sliced avocado, and cooked Bang Bang Shrimp.
3. Top with crumbled cotija or shredded cheddar cheese and a squeeze of lime juice.
4. Garnish with chopped cilantro if desired.
5. Serve immediately and enjoy these flavorful Bang Bang Shrimp tacos!

C. Bang Bang Shrimp Pasta
Ingredients:

- 1 pound spaghetti or linguine
- Cooked Bang Bang Shrimp (from the Traditional Bang Bang Shrimp recipe)
- 2 tablespoons olive oil
- 4 cloves garlic, minced
- 1/2 cup chicken or vegetable broth
- 1 cup heavy cream

- 1/4 cup grated Parmesan cheese
- Salt and pepper to taste
- Chopped fresh parsley for garnish

Instructions:

1. Cook pasta according to package instructions until al dente. Drain and set aside.
2. In a large skillet, heat olive oil over medium heat. Add minced garlic and sauté until fragrant, about 1 minute.
3. Pour in chicken or vegetable broth and bring to a simmer.
4. Stir in heavy cream and grated Parmesan cheese. Cook, stirring frequently, until the sauce thickens slightly, about 3-4 minutes.
5. Add cooked Bang Bang Shrimp to the sauce and stir to combine. Cook for an additional 2-3 minutes until shrimp are heated through.
6. Season with salt and pepper to taste.
7. Toss the cooked pasta with the Bang Bang Shrimp sauce until well coated.
8. Serve hot, garnished with chopped fresh parsley. Enjoy your creamy and flavorful Bang Bang Shrimp pasta!

D. Bang Bang Shrimp Lettuce Wraps
Ingredients:

- Cooked Bang Bang Shrimp (from the Traditional Bang Bang Shrimp recipe)
- Large lettuce leaves (such as iceberg or butter lettuce)
- Shredded carrots
- Thinly sliced cucumbers
- Cooked rice vermicelli noodles
- Chopped peanuts
- Fresh cilantro leaves

- Lime wedges
- Optional: additional Bang Bang sauce for drizzling

Instructions:

1. Prepare lettuce leaves by gently washing and patting them dry.
2. Place a spoonful of cooked rice vermicelli noodles onto each lettuce leaf.
3. Top with cooked Bang Bang Shrimp, shredded carrots, and thinly sliced cucumbers.
4. Garnish with chopped peanuts and fresh cilantro leaves.
5. Squeeze a lime wedge over each lettuce wrap before serving.
6. Optional: Drizzle additional Bang Bang sauce over the filling for extra flavor.
7. Roll up the lettuce leaves like a burrito, securing the filling inside.
8. Serve immediately and enjoy these refreshing and crunchy Bang Bang Shrimp lettuce wraps!

E. Bang Bang Shrimp Sandwiches
Ingredients:

- Cooked Bang Bang Shrimp (from the Traditional Bang Bang Shrimp recipe)
- Sandwich rolls or buns
- Shredded lettuce
- Sliced tomatoes
- Sliced red onions
- Sliced avocado
- Sliced pickles
- Mayonnaise
- Sriracha sauce
- Optional: additional Bang Bang sauce for drizzling

Instructions:

1. Split sandwich rolls or buns and lightly toast them, if desired.
2. Spread mayonnaise and Sriracha sauce on the bottom half of each roll.
3. Layer shredded lettuce, sliced tomatoes, red onions, avocado, and pickles on top of the sauce.
4. Add cooked Bang Bang Shrimp on top of the veggies.
5. Optional: Drizzle additional Bang Bang sauce over the shrimp for extra flavor.
6. Place the top half of the roll on top to complete the sandwich.
7. Serve immediately and enjoy these delicious and satisfying Bang Bang Shrimp sandwiches!

Chapter (3) Variations on Bang Bang Shrimp

A. Spicy Bang Bang Shrimp
Ingredients:

- Cooked Bang Bang Shrimp (from the Traditional Bang Bang Shrimp recipe)
- Extra hot sauce or chili flakes (adjust to taste)
- Sliced jalapeños (optional)
- Fresh chopped cilantro for garnish

Instructions:

1. Prepare the Bang Bang Shrimp following the Traditional Bang Bang Shrimp recipe.
2. Toss the cooked shrimp in additional hot sauce or sprinkle with chili flakes for an extra kick of heat.
3. Garnish with sliced jalapeños and fresh chopped cilantro.
4. Serve hot and enjoy these fiery Spicy Bang Bang Shrimp!

B. Grilled Bang Bang Shrimp Skewers
Ingredients:

- Cooked Bang Bang Shrimp (from the Traditional Bang Bang Shrimp recipe)
- Wooden or metal skewers
- Olive oil
- Salt and pepper to taste
- Fresh lime wedges for serving

Instructions:

1. Preheat grill to medium-high heat.
2. Thread cooked Bang Bang Shrimp onto skewers, leaving a little space between each shrimp.
3. Brush shrimp with olive oil and season with salt and pepper.
4. Grill shrimp skewers for 2-3 minutes on each side or until lightly charred.
5. Remove skewers from the grill and squeeze fresh lime juice over the shrimp.
6. Serve hot and enjoy these succulent Grilled Bang Bang Shrimp Skewers!

C. Bang Bang Shrimp Salad

Ingredients:

- Cooked Bang Bang Shrimp (from the Traditional Bang Bang Shrimp recipe)
- Mixed salad greens (such as lettuce, spinach, and arugula)
- Cherry tomatoes, halved
- Sliced cucumbers
- Sliced red onions
- Avocado slices
- Crumbled feta cheese
- Balsamic vinaigrette or your favorite dressing

Instructions:

1. In a large bowl, toss together mixed salad greens, cherry tomatoes, sliced cucumbers, red onions, avocado slices, and crumbled feta cheese.
2. Add cooked Bang Bang Shrimp on top of the salad.
3. Drizzle with balsamic vinaigrette or your favorite dressing.
4. Toss gently to combine.

5. Serve immediately and enjoy this refreshing Bang Bang Shrimp Salad!

D. Baked Bang Bang Shrimp
Ingredients:

- Cooked Bang Bang Shrimp (from the Traditional Bang Bang Shrimp recipe)
- Panko breadcrumbs
- Cooking spray or olive oil

Instructions:

1. Preheat the oven to 400°F (200°C).
2. Place cooked Bang Bang Shrimp on a baking sheet lined with parchment paper.
3. Sprinkle panko breadcrumbs over the shrimp, pressing gently to adhere.
4. Lightly spray the shrimp with cooking spray or drizzle with olive oil.
5. Bake in the preheated oven for 8-10 minutes or until the breadcrumbs are golden brown and the shrimp are heated through.
6. Remove from the oven and serve hot.
7. Enjoy these crispy and healthier Baked Bang Bang Shrimp as a guilt-free alternative to fried shrimp!

E. Bang Bang Shrimp Stir Fry
Ingredients:

- Cooked Bang Bang Shrimp (from the Traditional Bang Bang Shrimp recipe)
- Assorted vegetables (such as bell peppers, broccoli, snap peas, carrots, and mushrooms), sliced or chopped

- Olive oil or vegetable oil
- Soy sauce
- Minced garlic
- Fresh ginger, grated
- Red pepper flakes (optional)
- Cooked rice or noodles for serving

Instructions:

1. Heat olive oil or vegetable oil in a large skillet or wok over medium-high heat.
2. Add minced garlic and grated ginger to the skillet and cook for 1-2 minutes until fragrant.
3. Add assorted vegetables to the skillet and stir-fry for 3-4 minutes until tender-crisp.
4. Add cooked Bang Bang Shrimp to the skillet and toss with the vegetables.
5. Drizzle soy sauce over the shrimp and vegetables, tossing to coat evenly.
6. If desired, sprinkle with red pepper flakes for extra heat.
7. Continue to stir-fry for another 2-3 minutes until everything is heated through.
8. Serve hot over cooked rice or noodles.
9. Enjoy this quick and flavorful Bang Bang Shrimp Stir Fry as a delicious weeknight meal!

Chapter (4) Creative Bang Bang Shrimp Dishes

A. Bang Bang Shrimp Pizza

Ingredients:

- Pre-made pizza dough or pre-baked pizza crust
- Cooked Bang Bang Shrimp (from the Traditional Bang Bang Shrimp recipe)
- Pizza sauce
- Shredded mozzarella cheese
- Sliced red onions
- Sliced bell peppers
- Sliced jalapeños
- Fresh cilantro leaves
- Sriracha sauce (optional)

Instructions:

1. Preheat the oven to the temperature specified on the pizza dough or pre-baked pizza crust package.
2. Roll out the pizza dough onto a baking sheet or pizza stone.
3. Spread pizza sauce evenly over the dough.
4. Sprinkle shredded mozzarella cheese over the sauce.
5. Arrange cooked Bang Bang Shrimp, sliced red onions, bell peppers, and jalapeños on top of the cheese.
6. Bake in the preheated oven according to the pizza dough package instructions, until the crust is golden brown and the cheese is melted and bubbly.
7. Remove from the oven and garnish with fresh cilantro leaves.
8. Drizzle with Sriracha sauce for an extra kick of heat, if desired.
9. Slice and serve hot. Enjoy this unique and flavorful Bang Bang

Shrimp Pizza!

B. Bang Bang Shrimp Sushi Rolls
Ingredients:

- Sushi rice
- Nori seaweed sheets
- Cooked Bang Bang Shrimp (from the Traditional Bang Bang Shrimp recipe)
- Sliced avocado
- Sliced cucumber
- Sliced carrots
- Pickled ginger
- Wasabi
- Soy sauce

Instructions:

1. Prepare sushi rice according to package instructions and let it cool to room temperature.
2. Place a nori seaweed sheet on a sushi rolling mat.
3. Spread a thin layer of sushi rice over the nori, leaving a 1-inch border at the top edge.
4. Arrange cooked Bang Bang Shrimp, sliced avocado, cucumber, carrots, and pickled ginger in the center of the rice.
5. Roll the sushi tightly using the sushi mat, starting from the bottom edge and rolling towards the top edge.
6. Use a sharp knife to slice the sushi roll into bite-sized pieces.
7. Serve with wasabi and soy sauce for dipping.
8. Enjoy these delicious and inventive Bang Bang Shrimp Sushi Rolls!

C. Bang Bang Shrimp Nachos
Ingredients:

- Tortilla chips
- Cooked Bang Bang Shrimp (from the Traditional Bang Bang Shrimp recipe)
- Shredded Monterey Jack or cheddar cheese
- Black beans, drained and rinsed
- Diced tomatoes
- Sliced jalapeños
- Sliced green onions
- Sour cream
- Guacamole
- Salsa
- Chopped cilantro for garnish

Instructions:

1. Preheat the oven to 375°F (190°C).
2. Arrange tortilla chips in a single layer on a large baking sheet.
3. Sprinkle shredded cheese over the tortilla chips.
4. Top with cooked Bang Bang Shrimp, black beans, diced tomatoes, and sliced jalapeños.
5. Bake in the preheated oven for 8-10 minutes or until the cheese is melted and bubbly.
6. Remove from the oven and garnish with sliced green onions, dollops of sour cream, guacamole, salsa, and chopped cilantro.
7. Serve immediately and enjoy these irresistible Bang Bang Shrimp Nachos!

D. Bang Bang Shrimp Spring Rolls
  Ingredients:

- Rice paper wrappers
- Cooked Bang Bang Shrimp (from the Traditional Bang Bang

Shrimp recipe)
- Thin rice noodles, cooked according to package instructions
- Shredded lettuce
- Shredded carrots
- Sliced cucumber
- Fresh mint leaves
- Fresh cilantro leaves
- Dipping sauce of your choice (such as sweet chili sauce or peanut sauce)

Instructions:

1. Fill a shallow dish with warm water.
2. Dip a rice paper wrapper into the warm water for a few seconds until it becomes soft and pliable.
3. Place the softened rice paper wrapper on a clean work surface.
4. Arrange cooked Bang Bang Shrimp, rice noodles, shredded lettuce, shredded carrots, sliced cucumber, fresh mint leaves, and cilantro leaves in the center of the wrapper.
5. Fold the sides of the wrapper over the filling, then tightly roll it up, similar to a burrito.
6. Repeat with the remaining ingredients to make more spring rolls.
7. Serve the Bang Bang Shrimp Spring Rolls with your favorite dipping sauce.
8. Enjoy these light and flavorful spring rolls as a refreshing appetizer or snack!

E. Bang Bang Shrimp Sliders
Ingredients:

- Slider buns
- Cooked Bang Bang Shrimp (from the Traditional Bang Bang

Shrimp recipe)
- Shredded lettuce
- Sliced tomatoes
- Sliced red onions
- Sliced avocado
- Mayonnaise
- Sriracha sauce
- Optional: additional Bang Bang sauce for drizzling

Instructions:

1. Split slider buns and lightly toast them, if desired.
2. Spread mayonnaise and Sriracha sauce on the bottom half of each bun.
3. Layer shredded lettuce, sliced tomatoes, red onions, avocado slices, and cooked Bang Bang Shrimp on top of the sauce.
4. Optional: Drizzle additional Bang Bang sauce over the shrimp for extra flavor.
5. Place the top half of the bun on top to complete the sliders.
6. Serve immediately and enjoy these mouthwatering Bang Bang Shrimp Sliders!

Chapter (5) Sides and Accompaniments for Bang Bang Shrimp

A. Coconut Rice
Ingredients:

- 1 cup jasmine rice
- 1 cup coconut milk
- 1 cup water
- 1/2 teaspoon salt
- 1 tablespoon sugar (optional)
- Fresh cilantro for garnish (optional)

Instructions:

1. In a medium saucepan, combine jasmine rice, coconut milk, water, salt, and sugar (if using).
2. Bring the mixture to a boil over medium-high heat.
3. Once boiling, reduce the heat to low, cover, and simmer for 15-20 minutes, or until the liquid is absorbed and the rice is tender.
4. Fluff the rice with a fork and let it sit covered for an additional 5 minutes.
5. Garnish with fresh cilantro, if desired, before serving.
6. Serve hot alongside Bang Bang Shrimp for a delicious and fragrant pairing.

B. Garlic Butter Noodles
Ingredients:

- 8 ounces spaghetti or noodles of your choice

- 2 tablespoons butter
- 2 cloves garlic, minced
- Salt and pepper to taste
- Chopped parsley for garnish (optional)

Instructions:

1. Cook spaghetti or noodles according to package instructions until al dente. Drain and set aside.
2. In a large skillet, melt butter over medium heat.
3. Add minced garlic to the skillet and sauté for 1-2 minutes until fragrant.
4. Add the cooked spaghetti or noodles to the skillet and toss to coat evenly with the garlic butter.
5. Season with salt and pepper to taste.
6. Garnish with chopped parsley, if desired, before serving.
7. Serve hot as a tasty side dish alongside Bang Bang Shrimp.

C. Asian Slaw
Ingredients:

- 4 cups shredded cabbage (green or purple)
- 1 cup shredded carrots
- 1/4 cup chopped cilantro
- 2 green onions, thinly sliced
- 2 tablespoons rice vinegar
- 1 tablespoon soy sauce
- 1 tablespoon honey or sugar
- 1 tablespoon sesame oil
- Salt and pepper to taste
- Sesame seeds for garnish (optional)

Instructions:

1. In a large bowl, combine shredded cabbage, shredded carrots, chopped cilantro, and sliced green onions.
2. In a small bowl, whisk together rice vinegar, soy sauce, honey or sugar, sesame oil, salt, and pepper to make the dressing.
3. Pour the dressing over the cabbage mixture and toss to coat evenly.
4. Let the slaw sit for at least 15 minutes to allow the flavors to meld together.
5. Garnish with sesame seeds before serving, if desired.
6. Serve chilled as a refreshing and crunchy side dish with Bang Bang Shrimp.

D. Sweet Potato Fries
Ingredients:

- 2 large sweet potatoes, peeled and cut into fries
- 2 tablespoons olive oil
- 1 teaspoon paprika
- 1 teaspoon garlic powder
- 1/2 teaspoon salt
- 1/4 teaspoon black pepper

Instructions:

1. Preheat the oven to 425°F (220°C). Line a baking sheet with parchment paper.
2. In a large bowl, toss sweet potato fries with olive oil, paprika, garlic powder, salt, and black pepper until evenly coated.
3. Arrange the fries in a single layer on the prepared baking sheet.
4. Bake for 20-25 minutes, flipping halfway through, until the fries are crispy and golden brown.
5. Remove from the oven and let cool slightly before serving.
6. Serve hot as a sweet and savory side dish to complement Bang

Bang Shrimp.

E. Mango Avocado Salsa
Ingredients:

- 1 ripe mango, diced
- 1 ripe avocado, diced
- 1/4 cup red onion, finely chopped
- 1/4 cup fresh cilantro, chopped
- Juice of 1 lime
- Salt and pepper to taste

Instructions:

1. In a mixing bowl, combine diced mango, diced avocado, chopped red onion, and chopped cilantro.
2. Squeeze lime juice over the salsa and toss gently to combine.
3. Season with salt and pepper to taste.
4. Cover and refrigerate for at least 30 minutes to allow the flavors to meld together.
5. Serve chilled as a refreshing and fruity salsa alongside Bang Bang Shrimp.
6. Enjoy the vibrant flavors of mango and avocado in this delightful accompaniment.

Chapter (6) Sauces and Dips

A. Classic Bang Bang Sauce
Ingredients:

- 1/2 cup mayonnaise
- 2 tablespoons sweet chili sauce
- 1 tablespoon hot sauce (such as sriracha)
- 1 tablespoon honey
- 1 teaspoon lime juice
- 1/2 teaspoon garlic powder

Instructions:

1. In a small bowl, whisk together mayonnaise, sweet chili sauce, hot sauce, honey, lime juice, and garlic powder until smooth and well combined.
2. Taste and adjust the seasoning, adding more hot sauce for extra heat if desired.
3. Transfer the sauce to a serving dish.
4. Use as a dipping sauce for Bang Bang Shrimp or drizzle over dishes for added flavor.
5. Enjoy the creamy and spicy goodness of Classic Bang Bang Sauce!

B. Creamy Sriracha Dip
Ingredients:

- 1/2 cup mayonnaise
- 2 tablespoons sour cream
- 2 tablespoons sriracha sauce (adjust to taste)
- 1 tablespoon lime juice
- 1/2 teaspoon garlic powder

- Salt and pepper to taste

Instructions:

1. In a small bowl, whisk together mayonnaise, sour cream, sriracha sauce, lime juice, garlic powder, salt, and pepper until smooth and creamy.
2. Taste and adjust the seasoning, adding more sriracha sauce for extra heat if desired.
3. Transfer the dip to a serving bowl.
4. Serve as a dipping sauce for Bang Bang Shrimp or as a spicy condiment for other dishes.
5. Enjoy the creamy and tangy flavor of this irresistible Sriracha Dip!

C. Spicy Mango Salsa
Ingredients:

- 1 ripe mango, diced
- 1/2 red bell pepper, diced
- 1/4 cup red onion, finely chopped
- 1/4 cup fresh cilantro, chopped
- 1 jalapeño, seeded and minced
- Juice of 1 lime
- Salt and pepper to taste

Instructions:

1. In a mixing bowl, combine diced mango, diced red bell pepper, chopped red onion, minced jalapeño, and chopped cilantro.
2. Squeeze lime juice over the salsa and toss gently to combine.
3. Season with salt and pepper to taste.

4. Cover and refrigerate for at least 30 minutes to allow the flavors to meld together.
5. Serve chilled as a zesty salsa for Bang Bang Shrimp or as a refreshing topping for tacos, salads, or grilled meats.
6. Enjoy the sweet and spicy kick of Spicy Mango Salsa!

D. Sweet Chili Mayo
Ingredients:

- 1/2 cup mayonnaise
- 2 tablespoons sweet chili sauce
- 1 tablespoon honey
- 1 teaspoon lime juice
- 1/2 teaspoon garlic powder

Instructions:

1. In a small bowl, whisk together mayonnaise, sweet chili sauce, honey, lime juice, and garlic powder until smooth and well combined.
2. Taste and adjust the seasoning, adding more honey for sweetness or lime juice for tanginess if desired.
3. Transfer the sauce to a serving dish.
4. Use as a dipping sauce for Bang Bang Shrimp or as a delicious condiment for sandwiches, wraps, or burgers.
5. Enjoy the delightful combination of sweet and tangy flavors in this Sweet Chili Mayo!

E. Tangy Citrus Aioli
Ingredients:

- 1/2 cup mayonnaise
- 1 tablespoon fresh lemon juice
- 1 tablespoon fresh lime juice

- 1 teaspoon lemon zest
- 1 teaspoon lime zest
- 1 clove garlic, minced
- Salt and pepper to taste

Instructions:

1. In a small bowl, whisk together mayonnaise, fresh lemon juice, fresh lime juice, lemon zest, lime zest, minced garlic, salt, and pepper until smooth and creamy.
2. Taste and adjust the seasoning, adding more lemon juice or lime juice for extra tanginess if desired.
3. Transfer the aioli to a serving bowl.
4. Serve as a dipping sauce for Bang Bang Shrimp or as a zesty condiment for seafood, vegetables, or sandwiches.
5. Enjoy the vibrant citrus flavors of Tangy Citrus Aioli!

Chapter (7) Desserts with a Bang Bang Shrimp Twist

A. Bang Bang Shrimp Cakes with Vanilla Ice Cream

Ingredients:

- Cooked Bang Bang Shrimp (from the Traditional Bang Bang Shrimp recipe)
- 1 cup graham cracker crumbs
- 1/4 cup sweetened condensed milk
- Vanilla ice cream
- Caramel sauce (optional)
- Chopped nuts (optional)

Instructions:

1. In a mixing bowl, combine cooked Bang Bang Shrimp, graham cracker crumbs, and sweetened condensed milk. Mix until well combined.
2. Shape the mixture into small cakes or patties.
3. Heat a skillet over medium heat and lightly grease it with cooking spray or butter.
4. Cook the shrimp cakes for 2-3 minutes on each side until golden brown and heated through.
5. Serve the warm shrimp cakes with a scoop of vanilla ice cream.
6. Drizzle with caramel sauce and sprinkle with chopped nuts, if desired.
7. Enjoy the sweet and savory combination of Bang Bang Shrimp Cakes with Vanilla Ice Cream!

B. Bang Bang Shrimp Spring Roll Desserts

Ingredients:

- Cooked Bang Bang Shrimp (from the Traditional Bang Bang Shrimp recipe)
- Rice paper wrappers
- Sliced mango
- Sliced strawberries
- Fresh mint leaves
- Powdered sugar for dusting
- Chocolate sauce (optional)

Instructions:

1. Prepare a bowl of warm water for dipping the rice paper wrappers.
2. Dip a rice paper wrapper into the warm water for a few seconds until it becomes soft and pliable.
3. Place cooked Bang Bang Shrimp, sliced mango, sliced strawberries, and fresh mint leaves in the center of the wrapper.
4. Fold the sides of the wrapper over the filling, then tightly roll it up, similar to a burrito.
5. Repeat with the remaining ingredients to make more spring rolls.
6. Dust the spring rolls with powdered sugar before serving.
7. Drizzle with chocolate sauce for an extra indulgent treat, if desired.
8. Enjoy these refreshing and fruity Bang Bang Shrimp Spring Roll Desserts!

C. Bang Bang Shrimp Parfait
Ingredients:

- Cooked Bang Bang Shrimp (from the Traditional Bang Bang Shrimp recipe)
- Greek yogurt or vanilla pudding
- Granola
- Sliced bananas
- Sliced strawberries
- Honey or maple syrup
- Chopped nuts (optional)

Instructions:

1. In serving glasses or bowls, layer Greek yogurt or vanilla pudding, granola, sliced bananas, sliced strawberries, and cooked Bang Bang Shrimp.
2. Repeat the layers until the glasses are filled.
3. Drizzle honey or maple syrup over the top layer.
4. Garnish with chopped nuts, if desired.
5. Serve chilled and enjoy this unique and flavorful Bang Bang Shrimp Parfait!

D. Bang Bang Shrimp Mango Sorbet
Ingredients:

- 2 ripe mangoes, peeled and diced
- 1/4 cup honey or sugar
- Juice of 1 lime
- Cooked Bang Bang Shrimp (from the Traditional Bang Bang Shrimp recipe)

Instructions:

1. Place diced mangoes, honey or sugar, and lime juice in a blender or food processor.
2. Blend until smooth and creamy.

3. Transfer the mango mixture to a shallow dish and freeze for 4-6 hours, stirring occasionally, until firm.
4. Once the sorbet is frozen, scoop it into serving bowls or glasses.
5. Top each serving with a few pieces of cooked Bang Bang Shrimp.
6. Serve immediately and enjoy the refreshing and tropical flavors of Bang Bang Shrimp Mango Sorbet!

E. Bang Bang Shrimp Coconut Pudding
Ingredients:

- 1 can (13.5 oz) coconut milk
- 1/4 cup sugar
- 1/4 cup cornstarch
- Cooked Bang Bang Shrimp (from the Traditional Bang Bang Shrimp recipe)
- Shredded coconut for garnish

Instructions:

1. In a saucepan, combine coconut milk, sugar, and cornstarch. Whisk until smooth.
2. Place the saucepan over medium heat and cook, stirring constantly, until the mixture thickens and comes to a gentle boil.
3. Remove from heat and let the coconut pudding cool slightly.
4. Transfer the pudding to serving bowls or glasses and refrigerate until chilled and set.
5. Once the pudding is chilled, top each serving with a few pieces of cooked Bang Bang Shrimp.
6. Sprinkle shredded coconut over the top for garnish.
7. Serve cold and enjoy the creamy and tropical taste of Bang Bang Shrimp Coconut Pudding!

Chapter (8) Tips for Serving and Presentation

A. Garnishing Ideas

- Fresh herbs: Sprinkle chopped cilantro, parsley, or basil over Bang Bang Shrimp dishes for a pop of color and freshness.
- Citrus wedges: Serve lemon, lime, or orange wedges on the side to squeeze over the shrimp for a burst of citrus flavor.
- Sesame seeds: Sprinkle toasted sesame seeds over dishes like Bang Bang Shrimp Salad or Stir Fry for added texture and nuttiness.
- Thinly sliced green onions: Scatter sliced green onions over the top of dishes for a mild onion flavor and visual appeal.
- Edible flowers: Garnish plates with edible flowers such as nasturtiums or pansies for an elegant touch.

B. Pairing Suggestions

- Wine: Pair Bang Bang Shrimp with a crisp and refreshing white wine like Sauvignon Blanc or Pinot Grigio to complement the flavors of the shrimp.
- Beer: Opt for a light and citrusy beer such as a wheat beer or a pale ale to balance the spiciness of Bang Bang Shrimp.
- Cocktails: Serve Bang Bang Shrimp with a fruity cocktail like a mango margarita or a pineapple mojito for a tropical twist.
- Side dishes: Pair Bang Bang Shrimp with sides like coconut rice, garlic butter noodles, or Asian slaw to create a well-rounded and satisfying meal.

C. Plating Techniques

- Use colorful plates: Choose plates or platters in vibrant colors to make the Bang Bang Shrimp dishes visually appealing.
- Arrange food strategically: Place Bang Bang Shrimp and accompanying sides in an aesthetically pleasing arrangement on the plate, using different heights and textures for visual interest.
- Drizzle sauces artistically: Use a squeeze bottle or spoon to drizzle sauces like Classic Bang Bang Sauce or Sweet Chili Mayo in decorative patterns on the plate.
- Garnish with care: Place garnishes such as fresh herbs or citrus wedges delicately on top of the dishes to enhance their appearance without overwhelming the presentation.
- Consider symmetry: Aim for symmetry and balance when plating Bang Bang Shrimp dishes, arranging components evenly on the plate for a polished look.

Chapter (9) Brunch and Breakfast Bang Bang Shrimp

A. Bang Bang Shrimp Benedict
Ingredients:

- Cooked Bang Bang Shrimp (from the Traditional Bang Bang Shrimp recipe)
- English muffins, split and toasted
- Poached eggs
- Hollandaise sauce
- Chopped chives for garnish
- Optional: sliced avocado, tomato slices

Instructions:

1. Prepare the poached eggs and Hollandaise sauce according to your favorite recipes or using store-bought versions.
2. Top each toasted English muffin half with cooked Bang Bang Shrimp.
3. Place a poached egg on top of the shrimp.
4. Drizzle Hollandaise sauce generously over the eggs and shrimp.
5. Garnish with chopped chives.
6. Optionally, add slices of avocado and tomato on the side.
7. Serve immediately and enjoy this indulgent Bang Bang Shrimp Benedict for brunch!

B. Bang Bang Shrimp Breakfast Burritos
Ingredients:

- Cooked Bang Bang Shrimp (from the Traditional Bang Bang Shrimp recipe)
- Flour tortillas
- Scrambled eggs
- Shredded cheese (such as cheddar or Monterey Jack)
- Salsa
- Sliced avocado
- Sour cream
- Chopped cilantro for garnish

Instructions:

1. Warm the flour tortillas in a skillet or microwave.
2. Fill each tortilla with scrambled eggs, cooked Bang Bang Shrimp, shredded cheese, salsa, and sliced avocado.
3. Roll up the tortillas into burritos, tucking in the ends.
4. Place the burritos seam-side down on a serving plate.
5. Top with a dollop of sour cream and sprinkle with chopped cilantro.
6. Serve immediately and enjoy these flavorful Bang Bang Shrimp Breakfast Burritos!

C. Bang Bang Shrimp Hash
Ingredients:

- Cooked Bang Bang Shrimp (from the Traditional Bang Bang Shrimp recipe)
- Potatoes, diced and cooked (can use leftover roasted potatoes)
- Bell peppers, diced
- Onion, diced
- Garlic, minced
- Olive oil
- Salt and pepper to taste
- Optional: chopped fresh parsley or chives for garnish

Instructions:

1. Heat olive oil in a skillet over medium heat.
2. Add diced potatoes to the skillet and cook until golden brown and crispy.
3. Add diced bell peppers, onion, and minced garlic to the skillet. Cook until vegetables are tender.
4. Stir in cooked Bang Bang Shrimp and continue to cook until heated through.
5. Season with salt and pepper to taste.
6. Transfer the Bang Bang Shrimp hash to a serving dish.
7. Garnish with chopped fresh parsley or chives, if desired.
8. Serve hot and enjoy this hearty and satisfying Bang Bang Shrimp Hash for breakfast or brunch!

Chapter (10) Global Fusion Bang Bang Shrimp

A. Bang Bang Shrimp Curry
Ingredients:

- Cooked Bang Bang Shrimp (from the Traditional Bang Bang Shrimp recipe)
- 2 tablespoons vegetable oil
- 1 onion, finely chopped
- 2 cloves garlic, minced
- 1 tablespoon ginger, minced
- 2 tablespoons curry powder
- 1 can (14 ounces) coconut milk
- 1 tablespoon fish sauce
- 1 tablespoon soy sauce
- 1 tablespoon brown sugar
- Juice of 1 lime
- Salt and pepper to taste
- Fresh cilantro for garnish
- Cooked rice for serving

Instructions:

1. Heat vegetable oil in a large skillet over medium heat.
2. Add chopped onion and cook until softened, about 3-4 minutes.
3. Stir in minced garlic and ginger, and cook for another 1-2 minutes until fragrant.
4. Add curry powder to the skillet and cook, stirring constantly, for about 1 minute.
5. Pour in coconut milk, fish sauce, soy sauce, and brown sugar.

Stir to combine.

6. Bring the mixture to a simmer and let it cook for 5 minutes to allow the flavors to meld together.
7. Add cooked Bang Bang Shrimp to the skillet and stir to coat in the curry sauce. Cook for an additional 2-3 minutes until the shrimp are heated through.
8. Squeeze lime juice over the curry and season with salt and pepper to taste.
9. Serve the Bang Bang Shrimp Curry hot over cooked rice.
10. Garnish with fresh cilantro before serving.

B. Bang Bang Shrimp Tacos with a Twist
Ingredients:

- Cooked Bang Bang Shrimp (from the Traditional Bang Bang Shrimp recipe)
- 8 small flour or corn tortillas
- 1 cup coleslaw mix
- 1 avocado, sliced
- 1 lime, cut into wedges
- Sriracha mayo (1/4 cup mayonnaise mixed with 1 tablespoon sriracha sauce)
- Optional toppings: sliced jalapeños, chopped cilantro, diced tomatoes

Instructions:

1. Warm the tortillas in a skillet or microwave.
2. Fill each tortilla with coleslaw mix, sliced avocado, and cooked Bang Bang Shrimp.
3. Drizzle Sriracha mayo over the shrimp.
4. Squeeze lime juice over the tacos.
5. Top with optional toppings such as sliced jalapeños, chopped

cilantro, or diced tomatoes.
6. Serve the Bang Bang Shrimp Tacos with a Twist immediately.

C. Bang Bang Shrimp Ramen
Ingredients:

- Cooked Bang Bang Shrimp (from the Traditional Bang Bang Shrimp recipe)
- 4 cups chicken or vegetable broth
- 2 packs of instant ramen noodles
- 2 cups mixed vegetables (such as sliced mushrooms, bok choy, and shredded carrots)
- 2 tablespoons soy sauce
- 1 tablespoon fish sauce
- 1 tablespoon sriracha sauce (adjust to taste)
- 2 boiled eggs, halved
- Thinly sliced green onions for garnish
- Optional toppings: sesame seeds, nori seaweed

Instructions:

1. In a large pot, bring the chicken or vegetable broth to a boil.
2. Add instant ramen noodles and mixed vegetables to the pot. Cook according to the package instructions until noodles are tender.
3. Stir in soy sauce, fish sauce, and sriracha sauce.
4. Add cooked Bang Bang Shrimp to the pot and stir to combine.
5. Ladle the Bang Bang Shrimp Ramen into serving bowls.
6. Garnish with halved boiled eggs, thinly sliced green onions, sesame seeds, and nori seaweed.
7. Serve hot and enjoy this flavorful Bang Bang Shrimp Ramen.

Chapter (11) Healthy and Light Bang Bang Shrimp Options

A. Grilled Bang Bang Shrimp Salad with Citrus Dressing
Ingredients:

- Cooked Bang Bang Shrimp (from the Traditional Bang Bang Shrimp recipe)
- Mixed salad greens (such as spinach, arugula, and lettuce)
- Cherry tomatoes, halved
- Cucumber, sliced
- Red onion, thinly sliced
- Avocado, diced
- Citrus Dressing:
- Juice of 1 lemon
- Juice of 1 lime
- 2 tablespoons olive oil
- 1 teaspoon honey
- Salt and pepper to taste

Instructions:

1. Preheat a grill or grill pan over medium-high heat.
2. Thread cooked Bang Bang Shrimp onto skewers.
3. Grill the shrimp skewers for 2-3 minutes on each side until lightly charred and heated through.
4. In a large bowl, combine mixed salad greens, halved cherry tomatoes, sliced cucumber, thinly sliced red onion, and diced avocado.
5. In a small bowl, whisk together lemon juice, lime juice, olive oil, honey, salt, and pepper to make the citrus dressing.
6. Drizzle the citrus dressing over the salad and toss to coat evenly.

7. Divide the salad onto serving plates and top each with grilled Bang Bang Shrimp skewers.

8. Serve immediately and enjoy this light and refreshing Grilled Bang Bang Shrimp Salad with Citrus Dressing.

B. Bang Bang Shrimp Lettuce Cups
Ingredients:

- Cooked Bang Bang Shrimp (from the Traditional Bang Bang Shrimp recipe)
- Butter lettuce leaves
- Shredded carrots
- Sliced cucumber
- Chopped cilantro
- Chopped peanuts
- Bang Bang Sauce (from the Sauces and Dips section)

Instructions:

1. Wash and dry butter lettuce leaves, then arrange them on a serving platter.
2. Fill each lettuce cup with cooked Bang Bang Shrimp.
3. Top with shredded carrots, sliced cucumber, chopped cilantro, and chopped peanuts.
4. Drizzle Bang Bang Sauce over the top of each lettuce cup.
5. Serve immediately and enjoy these light and flavorful Bang Bang Shrimp Lettuce Cups.

C. Air-Fried Bang Bang Shrimp Bites
Ingredients:

- Cooked Bang Bang Shrimp (from the Traditional Bang Bang

Shrimp recipe)
- Panko breadcrumbs
- Olive oil spray
- Optional: Sriracha mayo or sweet chili sauce for dipping

Instructions:

1. Preheat the air fryer to 400°F (200°C).
2. Place cooked Bang Bang Shrimp on a plate.
3. Roll each shrimp in panko breadcrumbs until coated.
4. Arrange the breaded shrimp in a single layer in the air fryer basket.
5. Lightly spray the shrimp with olive oil spray.
6. Air fry for 5-7 minutes until the shrimp are crispy and golden brown.
7. Serve the Air-Fried Bang Bang Shrimp Bites immediately with Sriracha mayo or sweet chili sauce for dipping.
8. Enjoy these healthier and lighter Bang Bang Shrimp bites as a tasty appetizer or snack.

Chapter (12) Cocktails and Beverages Pairing

A. Spicy Mango Margarita
Ingredients:

- 2 oz tequila
- 1 oz triple sec or orange liqueur
- 1 oz fresh lime juice
- 2 oz mango nectar or puree
- 1/2 oz agave syrup
- 2-3 slices jalapeño (adjust to taste)
- Ice
- Salt or Tajin for rimming (optional)
- Lime wedges for garnish

Instructions:

1. Rim a glass with salt or Tajin by running a lime wedge around the rim and dipping it into salt or Tajin.
2. In a cocktail shaker, muddle jalapeño slices with lime juice and agave syrup.
3. Add tequila, triple sec, mango nectar or puree, and ice to the shaker.
4. Shake well until chilled.
5. Strain the mixture into the prepared glass filled with ice.
6. Garnish with a lime wedge.
7. Serve immediately and enjoy the Spicy Mango Margarita with Bang Bang Shrimp for a tropical and spicy pairing.

B. Coconut Pineapple Bang Bang Shrimp Cooler

Ingredients:

- 1 cup pineapple juice
- 1/2 cup coconut water
- 1/4 cup coconut cream
- 1 tablespoon lime juice
- Ice
- Pineapple slices for garnish

Instructions:

1. In a pitcher, combine pineapple juice, coconut water, coconut cream, and lime juice.
2. Stir well until the coconut cream is fully incorporated.
3. Fill glasses with ice.
4. Pour the coconut pineapple mixture over the ice.
5. Garnish with pineapple slices.
6. Serve immediately and enjoy the Coconut Pineapple Bang Bang Shrimp Cooler as a refreshing tropical drink to complement the flavors of Bang Bang Shrimp.

C. Ginger Lemongrass Bang Bang Shrimp Mocktail
Ingredients:

- 1 cup ginger beer
- 1/4 cup lemongrass syrup (made by simmering lemongrass stalks with equal parts water and sugar, then straining)
- 1/4 cup club soda
- Ice
- Lemongrass stalks for garnish

Instructions:

1. Fill glasses with ice.

2. In each glass, pour ginger beer and lemongrass syrup.
3. Top with club soda and stir gently to combine.
4. Garnish with lemongrass stalks.
5. Serve immediately and enjoy the refreshing and aromatic Ginger Lemongrass Bang Bang Shrimp Mocktail as a non-alcoholic option to pair with Bang Bang Shrimp.

Chapter (13) Family-Friendly Bang Bang Shrimp Meals

A. Bang Bang Shrimp Pizzas for Kids
Ingredients:

- Prepared pizza dough or pre-made pizza crusts
- Cooked Bang Bang Shrimp (from the Traditional Bang Bang Shrimp recipe)
- Pizza sauce
- Shredded mozzarella cheese
- Optional toppings: sliced bell peppers, sliced onions, sliced olives, sliced mushrooms, pineapple chunks

Instructions:

1. Preheat the oven according to the instructions on the pizza dough or crust packaging.
2. Roll out the pizza dough or place the pre-made crusts on a baking sheet.
3. Spread pizza sauce evenly over the dough or crusts.
4. Sprinkle shredded mozzarella cheese over the sauce.
5. Arrange cooked Bang Bang Shrimp and any desired toppings over the cheese.
6. Bake in the preheated oven according to the pizza dough or crust instructions until the crust is golden brown and the cheese is melted and bubbly.
7. Remove from the oven and let cool for a few minutes before slicing.
8. Serve the Bang Bang Shrimp Pizzas for Kids and let them enjoy creating their own pizza creations!

B. Bang Bang Shrimp Quesadillas

Ingredients:

- Flour tortillas
- Cooked Bang Bang Shrimp (from the Traditional Bang Bang Shrimp recipe)
- Shredded Monterey Jack or cheddar cheese
- Sliced green onions
- Optional: diced tomatoes, sliced jalapeños, sour cream, guacamole

Instructions:

1. Heat a non-stick skillet over medium heat.
2. Place a flour tortilla in the skillet.
3. Sprinkle shredded cheese over half of the tortilla.
4. Arrange cooked Bang Bang Shrimp and sliced green onions over the cheese.
5. Fold the tortilla in half to cover the filling, creating a quesadilla.
6. Cook for 2-3 minutes on each side until the tortilla is crispy and the cheese is melted.
7. Remove from the skillet and let cool for a minute before slicing into wedges.
8. Serve the Bang Bang Shrimp Quesadillas with optional toppings such as diced tomatoes, sliced jalapeños, sour cream, and guacamole.

C. Bang Bang Shrimp Mac and Cheese
Ingredients:

- Cooked Bang Bang Shrimp (from the Traditional Bang Bang Shrimp recipe)
- Macaroni pasta
- Butter
- All-purpose flour
- Milk
- Shredded cheddar cheese
- Salt and pepper to taste
- Optional: breadcrumbs for topping

Instructions:

1. Cook the macaroni pasta according to the package instructions. Drain and set aside.
2. In a saucepan, melt butter over medium heat.
3. Stir in an equal amount of all-purpose flour to make a roux.
4. Gradually whisk in milk until smooth and thickened.
5. Add shredded cheddar cheese to the sauce and stir until melted and smooth.
6. Season the cheese sauce with salt and pepper to taste.
7. Stir in cooked Bang Bang Shrimp and cooked macaroni pasta until well combined.
8. Transfer the Bang Bang Shrimp Mac and Cheese to a baking dish.
9. Optionally, sprinkle breadcrumbs over the top for a crispy topping.
10. Bake in a preheated oven at 350°F (175°C) for 20-25 minutes until bubbly and golden brown on top.
11. Serve the creamy and cheesy Bang Bang Shrimp Mac and Cheese for a comforting family meal.

Chapter (14) Holiday and Special Occasion Bang Bang Shrimp

A. Bang Bang Shrimp Christmas Appetizers
Bang Bang Shrimp Christmas Tree Appetizer:
Ingredients:

- Cooked Bang Bang Shrimp (from the Traditional Bang Bang Shrimp recipe)
- Wooden skewers
- Styrofoam cone
- Fresh parsley or cilantro leaves
- Grape or cherry tomatoes
- Optional: sliced bell peppers, olives, cheese cubes

Instructions:

1. Thread cooked Bang Bang Shrimp onto wooden skewers.
2. Insert the skewers into a styrofoam cone in a tree-like pattern.
3. Garnish the tree with fresh parsley or cilantro leaves to resemble branches.
4. Decorate the tree with grape or cherry tomatoes as ornaments.
5. Optionally, add sliced bell peppers, olives, or cheese cubes as additional decorations.
6. Serve the Bang Bang Shrimp Christmas Tree Appetizer as a festive and eye-catching holiday appetizer.

B. Bang Bang Shrimp Valentine's Day Dinner
Bang Bang Shrimp Valentine's Day Pasta:
Ingredients:

- Cooked Bang Bang Shrimp (from the Traditional Bang Bang Shrimp recipe)
- Linguine pasta
- Olive oil
- Garlic, minced
- Crushed red pepper flakes (optional)
- Cherry tomatoes, halved
- Fresh basil leaves, chopped
- Grated Parmesan cheese
- Salt and pepper to taste

Instructions:

1. Cook linguine pasta according to the package instructions. Drain and set aside.
2. In a large skillet, heat olive oil over medium heat.
3. Add minced garlic and crushed red pepper flakes (if using) to the skillet. Cook until fragrant.
4. Add cherry tomatoes to the skillet and cook until softened.
5. Stir in cooked Bang Bang Shrimp and chopped fresh basil leaves.
6. Add the cooked linguine pasta to the skillet and toss to coat evenly.
7. Season with salt and pepper to taste.
8. Serve the Bang Bang Shrimp Valentine's Day Pasta with grated Parmesan cheese on top for a romantic dinner.

C. Bang Bang Shrimp Easter Brunch Delights
Bang Bang Shrimp Easter Brunch Frittata:
Ingredients:

- Cooked Bang Bang Shrimp (from the Traditional Bang Bang Shrimp recipe)

- Eggs
- Milk or cream
- Salt and pepper to taste
- Olive oil
- Chopped bell peppers
- Chopped onions
- Spinach leaves
- Shredded cheese (such as cheddar or mozzarella)

Instructions:

1. Preheat the oven to 350°F (175°C).
2. In a bowl, whisk together eggs, milk or cream, salt, and pepper.
3. Heat olive oil in an oven-safe skillet over medium heat.
4. Add chopped bell peppers and onions to the skillet. Cook until softened.
5. Add spinach leaves to the skillet and cook until wilted.
6. Pour the egg mixture into the skillet, covering the vegetables.
7. Scatter cooked Bang Bang Shrimp evenly over the top.
8. Sprinkle shredded cheese over the frittata.
9. Transfer the skillet to the preheated oven and bake for 20-25 minutes until the eggs are set and the cheese is melted and bubbly.
10. Remove from the oven and let cool for a few minutes before slicing.
11. Serve the Bang Bang Shrimp Easter Brunch Frittata as a delicious and satisfying Easter brunch dish.

Chapter (15) Cooking with Leftover Bang Bang Shrimp

A. Bang Bang Shrimp Rice Bowls
Ingredients:

- Leftover Bang Bang Shrimp (from the Traditional Bang Bang Shrimp recipe)
- Cooked rice (white or brown)
- Sliced avocado
- Shredded lettuce or mixed greens
- Sliced cucumbers
- Sliced carrots
- Soy sauce or teriyaki sauce for drizzling
- Optional toppings: sliced green onions, sesame seeds, Sriracha mayo

Instructions:

1. Reheat leftover Bang Bang Shrimp in a skillet over medium heat until heated through.
2. Divide cooked rice among serving bowls.
3. Top each bowl with reheated Bang Bang Shrimp.
4. Arrange sliced avocado, shredded lettuce or mixed greens, sliced cucumbers, and sliced carrots around the shrimp.
5. Drizzle soy sauce or teriyaki sauce over the rice bowl.
6. Optionally, garnish with sliced green onions, sesame seeds, and a dollop of Sriracha mayo.
7. Serve the Bang Bang Shrimp Rice Bowls hot and enjoy this flavorful and satisfying meal.

B. Bang Bang Shrimp Stuffed Peppers
Ingredients:

- Leftover Bang Bang Shrimp (from the Traditional Bang Bang Shrimp recipe)
- Bell peppers (any color), halved and seeded
- Cooked quinoa or rice
- Shredded cheese (such as cheddar or Monterey Jack)
- Chopped cilantro for garnish
- Optional toppings: sliced avocado, sour cream, salsa

Instructions:

1. Preheat the oven to 375°F (190°C).
2. Arrange halved and seeded bell peppers in a baking dish.
3. Fill each bell pepper half with cooked quinoa or rice.
4. Top the quinoa or rice with leftover Bang Bang Shrimp.
5. Sprinkle shredded cheese over the shrimp.
6. Bake in the preheated oven for 20-25 minutes until the peppers are tender and the cheese is melted and bubbly.
7. Remove from the oven and let cool for a few minutes.
8. Garnish with chopped cilantro and optional toppings such as sliced avocado, sour cream, and salsa.
9. Serve the Bang Bang Shrimp Stuffed Peppers as a delicious and nutritious meal.

C. Bang Bang Shrimp Omelette
Ingredients:

- Leftover Bang Bang Shrimp (from the Traditional Bang Bang Shrimp recipe)
- Eggs
- Milk or cream
- Salt and pepper to taste
- Butter or oil for cooking
- Shredded cheese (such as cheddar or mozzarella)
- Chopped green onions for garnish

Instructions:

1. In a bowl, whisk together eggs, milk or cream, salt, and pepper.
2. Heat butter or oil in a non-stick skillet over medium heat.
3. Pour the egg mixture into the skillet and let it set slightly.
4. Arrange leftover Bang Bang Shrimp on one half of the omelette.
5. Sprinkle shredded cheese over the shrimp.
6. Fold the other half of the omelette over the filling.
7. Cook for a few more minutes until the cheese is melted and the omelette is cooked through.
8. Slide the omelette onto a serving plate.
9. Garnish with chopped green onions.
10. Serve the Bang Bang Shrimp Omelette hot and enjoy this quick and easy breakfast or brunch option.

Chapter (16) Gluten-Free Bang Bang Shrimp Recipes

A. Gluten-Free Bang Bang Shrimp Noodles
Ingredients:

- Gluten-free noodles (such as rice noodles or gluten-free spaghetti)
- Cooked Bang Bang Shrimp (from the Traditional Bang Bang Shrimp recipe)
- Sliced bell peppers
- Sliced carrots
- Chopped green onions
- Gluten-free Bang Bang Sauce (from the Sauces and Dips section)

Instructions:

1. Cook gluten-free noodles according to the package instructions. Drain and set aside.
2. In a skillet, heat cooked Bang Bang Shrimp until heated through.
3. Add sliced bell peppers and sliced carrots to the skillet. Cook until vegetables are tender-crisp.
4. Add cooked gluten-free noodles to the skillet and toss to combine.
5. Pour gluten-free Bang Bang Sauce over the noodles and shrimp mixture. Stir well to coat evenly.
6. Garnish with chopped green onions.
7. Serve the Gluten-Free Bang Bang Shrimp Noodles hot and enjoy this flavorful and gluten-free dish.

B. Bang Bang Shrimp Lettuce Wraps (Gluten-Free Version)
Ingredients:

- Lettuce leaves (such as butter lettuce or iceberg lettuce)
- Cooked Bang Bang Shrimp (from the Traditional Bang Bang Shrimp recipe)
- Shredded cabbage or coleslaw mix
- Sliced cucumbers
- Shredded carrots
- Chopped cilantro
- Gluten-free Bang Bang Sauce (from the Sauces and Dips section)

Instructions:

1. Wash and dry lettuce leaves, then arrange them on a serving platter.
2. Fill each lettuce leaf with cooked Bang Bang Shrimp.
3. Top with shredded cabbage or coleslaw mix, sliced cucumbers, shredded carrots, and chopped cilantro.
4. Drizzle gluten-free Bang Bang Sauce over the top.
5. Serve the Bang Bang Shrimp Lettuce Wraps immediately and enjoy this light and gluten-free version.

C. Gluten-Free Bang Bang Shrimp Pizza Crust
Ingredients:

- Gluten-free pizza crust mix
- Cooked Bang Bang Shrimp (from the Traditional Bang Bang Shrimp recipe)
- Pizza sauce (gluten-free)
- Shredded mozzarella cheese (gluten-free)
- Sliced bell peppers
- Sliced onions

- Gluten-free Bang Bang Sauce (from the Sauces and Dips section)

Instructions:

1. Prepare gluten-free pizza crust according to the package instructions.
2. Spread gluten-free pizza sauce evenly over the crust.
3. Sprinkle shredded mozzarella cheese over the sauce.
4. Top with cooked Bang Bang Shrimp, sliced bell peppers, and sliced onions.
5. Drizzle gluten-free Bang Bang Sauce over the top.
6. Bake in a preheated oven according to the pizza crust instructions until the crust is golden brown and the cheese is melted and bubbly.
7. Remove from the oven and let cool for a few minutes before slicing.
8. Serve the Gluten-Free Bang Bang Shrimp Pizza hot and enjoy this gluten-free twist on a classic favorite.

Chapter (17) Vegan and Vegetarian Bang Bang Shrimp Alternatives

A. Crispy Tofu "Bang Bang Shrimp"
Ingredients:

- Firm tofu, pressed and cut into cubes
- Cornstarch
- Oil for frying
- Vegan Bang Bang Sauce (from the Sauces and Dips section)
- Optional: chopped green onions for garnish, sesame seeds

Instructions:

1. Press tofu to remove excess moisture, then cut into cubes.
2. Coat tofu cubes in cornstarch.
3. Heat oil in a skillet over medium-high heat.
4. Fry tofu cubes until golden brown and crispy.
5. Remove tofu from the skillet and drain on paper towels.
6. Toss crispy tofu cubes in vegan Bang Bang Sauce until coated.
7. Garnish with chopped green onions and sesame seeds if desired.
8. Serve the Crispy Tofu "Bang Bang Shrimp" hot and enjoy this vegan alternative.

B. Bang Bang Cauliflower Bites
Ingredients:

- Cauliflower florets
- Gluten-free flour or all-purpose flour (for a non-vegan option)
- Plant-based milk (such as almond milk or soy milk)
- Bread crumbs (gluten-free if needed)
- Oil for frying or baking
- Vegan Bang Bang Sauce (from the Sauces and Dips section)

- Optional: chopped cilantro or parsley for garnish, lime wedges

Instructions:

1. Preheat oven to 425°F (220°C) if baking.
2. In separate bowls, place flour, plant-based milk, and bread crumbs.
3. Dip cauliflower florets into flour, then plant-based milk, and finally bread crumbs, coating evenly.
4. For frying: Heat oil in a skillet over medium-high heat. Fry cauliflower florets until golden brown and crispy. Drain on paper towels.
5. For baking: Place breaded cauliflower florets on a baking sheet lined with parchment paper. Bake for 20-25 minutes until golden brown and crispy.
6. Toss fried or baked cauliflower florets in vegan Bang Bang Sauce until coated.
7. Garnish with chopped cilantro or parsley and serve with lime wedges if desired.
8. Serve the Bang Bang Cauliflower Bites hot and enjoy this vegan-friendly appetizer or snack.

C. Vegan Bang Bang Shrimp Sushi
Ingredients:

- Sushi rice
- Nori seaweed sheets
- Cooked Bang Bang Cauliflower Bites (from recipe B)
- Sliced avocado
- Sliced cucumber
- Vegan Bang Bang Sauce (from the Sauces and Dips section)
- Sesame seeds
- Soy sauce, wasabi, and pickled ginger for serving

Instructions:

1. Prepare sushi rice according to package instructions and let it cool.
2. Place a nori seaweed sheet on a sushi rolling mat.
3. Spread a thin layer of sushi rice evenly over the nori sheet, leaving a small border at the top.
4. Arrange cooked Bang Bang Cauliflower Bites, sliced avocado, and sliced cucumber in a line across the center of the rice.
5. Drizzle vegan Bang Bang Sauce over the filling.
6. Roll up the sushi tightly using the sushi rolling mat.
7. Slice the sushi roll into bite-sized pieces using a sharp knife.
8. Sprinkle sesame seeds over the sushi rolls.
9. Serve the Vegan Bang Bang Shrimp Sushi with soy sauce, wasabi, and pickled ginger.

Chapter (18) Quick and Easy Bang Bang Shrimp Appetizers

A. Bang Bang Shrimp Wonton Cups

Ingredients:

- Wonton wrappers
- Cooking spray
- Cooked Bang Bang Shrimp (from the Traditional Bang Bang Shrimp recipe)
- Shredded lettuce or mixed greens
- Diced tomatoes
- Chopped green onions
- Bang Bang Sauce (from the Sauces and Dips section)
- Optional: sesame seeds for garnish

Instructions:

1. Preheat the oven to 375°F (190°C).
2. Lightly spray a mini muffin tin with cooking spray.
3. Press wonton wrappers into the muffin tin to form cups.
4. Bake in the preheated oven for 5-7 minutes until golden brown and crispy.
5. Remove the wonton cups from the muffin tin and let cool slightly.
6. Fill each wonton cup with shredded lettuce or mixed greens.
7. Top with cooked Bang Bang Shrimp.
8. Garnish with diced tomatoes and chopped green onions.
9. Drizzle Bang Bang Sauce over the top.
10. Optionally, sprinkle sesame seeds for garnish.
11. Serve the Bang Bang Shrimp Wonton Cups as a delightful and easy appetizer for any occasion.

B. Bang Bang Shrimp Stuffed Mushrooms
Ingredients:

- Large mushrooms, stems removed
- Cooked Bang Bang Shrimp (from the Traditional Bang Bang Shrimp recipe)
- Cream cheese (regular or vegan), softened
- Chopped green onions
- Bang Bang Sauce (from the Sauces and Dips section)
- Optional: breadcrumbs for topping

Instructions:

1. Preheat the oven to 375°F (190°C).
2. Place mushroom caps on a baking sheet lined with parchment paper.
3. In a bowl, mix together cooked Bang Bang Shrimp, softened cream cheese, and chopped green onions.
4. Stuff each mushroom cap with the Bang Bang Shrimp mixture.
5. Drizzle Bang Bang Sauce over the stuffed mushrooms.
6. Optionally, sprinkle breadcrumbs over the top for a crispy topping.
7. Bake in the preheated oven for 15-20 minutes until mushrooms are tender and filling is heated through.
8. Remove from the oven and let cool for a few minutes before serving.
9. Serve the Bang Bang Shrimp Stuffed Mushrooms as a savory and indulgent appetizer.

C. Bang Bang Shrimp Crostini
Ingredients:

- Baguette, sliced
- Olive oil
- Cooked Bang Bang Shrimp (from the Traditional Bang Bang Shrimp recipe)
- Chopped fresh parsley or cilantro
- Bang Bang Sauce (from the Sauces and Dips section)
- Optional: grated Parmesan cheese

Instructions:

1. Preheat the oven to 375°F (190°C).
2. Arrange baguette slices on a baking sheet.
3. Brush each slice with olive oil.
4. Bake in the preheated oven for 5-7 minutes until golden brown and crispy.
5. Remove from the oven and let cool slightly.
6. Top each crostini with cooked Bang Bang Shrimp.
7. Drizzle Bang Bang Sauce over the shrimp.
8. Garnish with chopped fresh parsley or cilantro.
9. Optionally, sprinkle grated Parmesan cheese over the top.
10. Serve the Bang Bang Shrimp Crostini as an elegant and flavorful appetizer option.

Chapter (19) Cooking for a Crowd: Bang Bang Shrimp Party Platters

A. Bang Bang Shrimp Skewer Platter

Ingredients:

- Cooked Bang Bang Shrimp (from the Traditional Bang Bang Shrimp recipe)
- Wooden skewers
- Mixed greens or shredded lettuce
- Cherry tomatoes
- Sliced cucumbers
- Sliced bell peppers
- Bang Bang Sauce (from the Sauces and Dips section)
- Optional: lemon wedges for garnish

Instructions:

1. Thread cooked Bang Bang Shrimp onto wooden skewers.
2. Arrange mixed greens or shredded lettuce on a large platter.
3. Place skewers of Bang Bang Shrimp on top of the greens.
4. Scatter cherry tomatoes, sliced cucumbers, and sliced bell peppers around the shrimp skewers.
5. Serve Bang Bang Sauce in a bowl alongside the platter for dipping.
6. Garnish with lemon wedges for added freshness.
7. Serve the Bang Bang Shrimp Skewer Platter as a colorful and flavorful appetizer option for your party guests.

B. Bang Bang Shrimp Slider Station

Ingredients:

- Mini slider buns
- Cooked Bang Bang Shrimp (from the Traditional Bang Bang Shrimp recipe)
- Shredded lettuce
- Sliced tomatoes
- Sliced avocado
- Bang Bang Sauce (from the Sauces and Dips section)
- Optional: sliced red onions, pickles

Instructions:

1. Arrange mini slider buns on a large serving platter.
2. Fill each bun with cooked Bang Bang Shrimp.
3. Top with shredded lettuce, sliced tomatoes, and sliced avocado.
4. Drizzle Bang Bang Sauce over the shrimp.
5. Optionally, add sliced red onions and pickles as additional toppings.
6. Serve the Bang Bang Shrimp Slider Station with toothpicks for easy serving.
7. Let your guests customize their sliders with their favorite toppings.

C. Bang Bang Shrimp Nacho Bar
Ingredients:

- Tortilla chips (assorted varieties)
- Cooked Bang Bang Shrimp (from the Traditional Bang Bang Shrimp recipe)
- Shredded cheese (such as cheddar or Monterey Jack)
- Sliced jalapeños
- Diced tomatoes
- Sliced black olives
- Guacamole

- Sour cream
- Salsa
- Bang Bang Sauce (from the Sauces and Dips section)
- Optional: chopped cilantro, diced onions, corn kernels

Instructions:

1. Arrange assorted tortilla chips on a large platter or serving tray.
2. Scatter cooked Bang Bang Shrimp over the chips.
3. Sprinkle shredded cheese over the shrimp and chips.
4. Top with sliced jalapeños, diced tomatoes, sliced black olives, and any other desired toppings.
5. Serve guacamole, sour cream, salsa, and Bang Bang Sauce in separate bowls alongside the platter.
6. Optionally, garnish with chopped cilantro, diced onions, and corn kernels for added flavor and texture.
7. Let your guests build their own Bang Bang Shrimp nachos according to their preferences.

Chapter (20) Preserving the Bang Bang Shrimp Experience: Canning and Pickling

A. Pickled Bang Bang Shrimp
  Ingredients:

- Cooked Bang Bang Shrimp (from the Traditional Bang Bang Shrimp recipe)
- White vinegar
- Water
- Sugar
- Salt
- Peppercorns
- Bay leaves
- Garlic cloves
- Red chili flakes (optional)

Instructions:

1. Prepare a pickling brine by combining equal parts white vinegar and water in a saucepan. Add sugar, salt, peppercorns, bay leaves, garlic cloves, and red chili flakes (if using). Bring to a boil and simmer for 5 minutes.
2. Pack cooked Bang Bang Shrimp into sterilized canning jars.
3. Pour the hot pickling brine over the shrimp, ensuring they are completely covered.
4. Seal the jars tightly with lids and rings.
5. Process the jars in a boiling water bath for the recommended time according to your altitude and jar size.
6. Allow the pickled Bang Bang Shrimp to cool completely before storing in a cool, dark place.
7. Let the flavors develop for at least a week before enjoying.

B. Bang Bang Shrimp Relish
Ingredients:

- Cooked Bang Bang Shrimp (from the Traditional Bang Bang Shrimp recipe)
- Red bell peppers, diced
- Red onion, diced
- Cucumber, diced
- Rice vinegar
- Sugar
- Salt
- Red chili flakes (optional)
- Fresh cilantro, chopped

Instructions:

1. In a mixing bowl, combine diced red bell peppers, red onion, cucumber, and cooked Bang Bang Shrimp.
2. In a small saucepan, heat rice vinegar, sugar, salt, and red chili flakes (if using) until the sugar is dissolved.
3. Pour the hot vinegar mixture over the shrimp and vegetable mixture.
4. Stir in chopped fresh cilantro.
5. Let the Bang Bang Shrimp relish cool to room temperature before transferring it to sterilized jars.
6. Store the relish in the refrigerator for up to 2 weeks.
7. Serve the Bang Bang Shrimp Relish as a tangy and flavorful condiment for grilled meats, sandwiches, or salads.

C. Bang Bang Shrimp Chutney
Ingredients:

- Cooked Bang Bang Shrimp (from the Traditional Bang Bang Shrimp recipe)

- Mango, peeled and diced
- Red onion, diced
- Apple cider vinegar
- Brown sugar
- Ground ginger
- Ground cinnamon
- Ground cloves
- Salt

Instructions:

1. In a saucepan, combine diced mango, red onion, apple cider vinegar, brown sugar, ground ginger, ground cinnamon, ground cloves, and salt.
2. Bring the mixture to a boil, then reduce the heat and simmer for about 20 minutes until the mango and onion are softened and the mixture has thickened.
3. Stir in cooked Bang Bang Shrimp and continue to cook for another 5 minutes.
4. Let the Bang Bang Shrimp chutney cool to room temperature before transferring it to sterilized jars.
5. Store the chutney in the refrigerator for up to 2 weeks.
6. Serve the Bang Bang Shrimp Chutney as a delightful accompaniment to grilled seafood, chicken, or as a topping for crackers or crostini.

❖ Conclusion

A. Final Thoughts on Bang Bang Shrimp

Bang Bang Shrimp is truly a culinary delight, offering a perfect balance of flavors and textures that tantalize the taste buds. From its crispy coating to its creamy and spicy sauce, Bang Bang Shrimp never fails to impress with its irresistible combination of sweet, savory, and tangy elements. Whether enjoyed as a classic appetizer, a creative fusion dish, or a flavorful topping, Bang Bang Shrimp always leaves a lasting impression on those who indulge in its deliciousness.

B. Encouragement for Culinary Exploration

As you journey through the world of Bang Bang Shrimp, we encourage you to unleash your creativity and explore the endless possibilities it offers. Don't be afraid to experiment with different ingredients, flavors, and cooking techniques to make each dish uniquely your own. Whether you're hosting a casual gathering or a special occasion, Bang Bang Shrimp is sure to elevate any meal and leave your guests craving for more.

C. Thank You and Enjoy Your Bangin' Shrimp Creations!

We sincerely thank you for joining us on this culinary adventure filled with Bang Bang Shrimp delights. We hope this cookbook has inspired you to embark on your own flavorful journey and create unforgettable moments around the dining table. From traditional favorites to innovative creations, may your Bang Bang Shrimp creations always bring joy and satisfaction to those you share them with. Bon appétit!